musée
# YVES SAINT LAURENT
marrakech

Éditions Jardin Majorelle

*"When Yves Saint Laurent first discovered
Marrakech in 1966,
he was so moved by the city that
he immediately decided to buy a house here,
and returned regularly.
It feels perfectly natural, fifty years later,
to build a museum dedicated to his oeuvre,
which was so inspired by this country."*

PIERRE BERGÉ

Pierre Bergé
and Yves Saint Laurent
at the Menara Gardens,
Marrakech

# FOREWORD

In the annals of fashion history, the Maison Yves Saint Laurent remains unique in its impressive trajectory; one that resulted from the unmatched youthful talent of the couturier and his uncanny ability to mirror and accompany his generation. From those early years of the couture house, Yves Saint Laurent and his partner Pierre Bergé had the far-reaching vision —which was precursory— of safeguarding original models, sketches, patterns, and accessories, thus creating the basis for the Pierre Bergé-Yves Saint Laurent Foundation's inimitable archives and reserves, which today remain unparalleled and are unlike any counterparts in the world of fashion.

Concurrent with the opening of the Musée Yves Saint Laurent Paris, the Fondation Pierre Bergé–Yves Saint Laurent has overseen the creation of another museum in Marrakech (mYSLm) in partnership with the Fondation Jardin Majorelle. It opens its doors in the Moroccan city beloved by both the great couturier and Pierre Bergé. Adjacent to the fabled Jardin Majorelle, which was saved from destruction by Yves Saint Laurent and Pierre Bergé in 1980, the mYSLm will not only exhibit the couturier's creations, but will offer both the Marrakech community and the city's visiting tourists diverse cultural experiences via a temporary exhibition hall, a large auditorium —for film projections, concerts and symposiums—, and a reference library devoted to the various fields associated with the Jardin Majorelle, including Berber history, botany, Moorish-Andalusian culture and, of course, fashion.

This museum that bears his name places Yves Saint Laurent in a historical context, yet is anchored in the present and looks towards the future, promoting an inter-disciplinary culture that is as universal and vibrant as the couturier's legacy.

**MADISON COX**
PRESIDENT OF THE FONDATION JARDIN MAJORELLE, MARRAKECH
AND THE FONDATION PIERRE BERGÉ – YVES SAINT LAURENT, PARIS

*"We immediately fell in love with the city,
the people, this country. We were
so enamoured that at the end of our stay,
in the plane taking us home,
we already had a binding sales agreement
in our hands for the house we would purchase
in the medina —Dar El Hanch
(The House of the Serpent).
It's when our passion for Morocco began."*

YVES SAINT LAURENT

Yves Saint Laurent
at the Palmeraie,
Marrakech

# YVES SAINT LAURENT
# AND MOROCCO

Yves Saint Laurent did not consider Morocco a destination, but rather an Eden, a revelation. Since the first time he set foot there, in 1966, it was love at first sight. The couturier was continually inspired by the rose-coloured mountains beyond the Ourika Valley and the green ceramic tiles that adorn the walls and minarets of the mosques. The bustling marketplaces, the vistas that seemed to leap from Matisse's *Paysage vu de la Fenêtre* and *Marabout*, would become dresses or coats trimmed with passementerie, worn with fez.

Yves Saint Laurent's Morocco evolved from this proliferation of natural tones and powerful colours found only in nature and in art: Delacroix reds, Majorelle blues, the green marble of Agadir, the yellow windows, the turquoise pergolas, all in a dizzying explosion of fragrances, plants and flowers, gold-coloured bamboos, mauve-winged insects, eucalyptus and orange trees, and palms...a luxuriant nature that reminds one of the Villa Brooks in Tangier, so dear to Matisse: "...the garden is an absolute reservoir of abstract colours; one no longer has the impression of making any effort in transposing nature to canvas." Idealised in the Fall-Winter 1976 "Opéra–Ballets Russes" collection, Yves Saint Laurent's Morocco is a palette of sensations and colours, "those of the earth, of the sand, but also those of the street, of women in turquoise and mauve caftans, the colours of the sky..."

Every winter, Yves Saint Laurent would return to Marrakech to immerse himself once again in a "magical, rose and peaceful atmosphere." He would leave carrying marvellous sketches. In Marrakech, the house built by Jacques Majorelle, son of the renowned cabinetmaker from Nancy, was initially called "Bou Saf Saf", meaning "the poplars" in Arabic. Upon acquiring it, Yves Saint Laurent and Pierre Bergé renamed this Orientalist treasure trove the "Villa Oasis". One is immersed in a décor where everything is "luxury, calm and voluptuousness": doors of sculpted cedar wood, *zellige* ceramic tiles, Syrian cupboards inlaid with mother-of-pearl, exquisite carpets, *mashrabiya* armchairs, precious Art Deco furniture and objects. The magic continues in the exotic garden, in such a way that its trees and flowers bear witness to the shimmering reflection of dresses in movement, and are indeed their domineering spirit and everlasting descendants.

**LAURENCE BENAÏM**
JOURNALIST, WRITER, AND AUTHOR OF NUMEROUS BOOKS
DEVOTED TO YVES SAINT LAURENT

Yves Saint Laurent
at the Jemaa El Fna Square
and in the medina of
Marrakech.

12

Pierre Bergé, Yves Saint
Laurent and Talitha Getty,
Marrakech

—

Tamy Tazi and Yves Saint
Laurent, Marrakech

—

Yves Saint Laurent and
Bianca Jagger, Marrakech

Yves Saint Laurent
with François and Betty
Catroux, Marrakech

—

Pierre Bergé
and Yves Saint Laurent
at the Jardin Majorelle,
Marrakech

Salon at the Villa Oasis,
Marrakech, built by
Jacques Majorelle in 1924;
acquired and restored
by Pierre Bergé
and Yves Saint Laurent
in 1980

—

The painter Jacques
Majorelle's studio
which today houses
the Berber Museum
at the Jardin Majorelle

Reproduction of a wall
mural painted by
Yves Saint Laurent
in the dining room of
Dar El Hanch ("The House
of the Serpent" in Arabic),
the first house acquired
by the couturier
and Pierre Bergé
in Marrakech in 1966

*"In Morocco, I realised that the range*
*of colours I use was that*
*of the zelliges, zouacs, djellabas and caftans.*
*The boldness seen since then in my work,*
*I owe to this country, to its forceful harmonies,*
*to its audacious combinations,*
*to the fervour of its creativity.*
*This culture became mine, but I wasn't satisfied*
*with absorbing it;*
*I transformed and adapted it."*

**YVES SAINT LAURENT**

The 1983 exhibition
*Yves Saint Laurent –
25 Years of Design* at
the Metropolitan Museum
of Art in New York

*"Why Yves Saint Laurent?
Because he is a genius, because he knows
everything about women."*

**DIANA VREELAND**

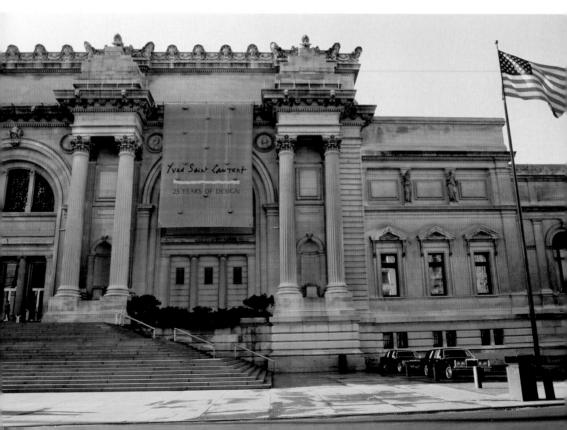

# AN ESSENTIAL EDEN

Yves Saint Laurent was the first living fashion designer to enjoy worldwide exhibitions dedicated to his work, beginning in 1983 with a major retrospective at The Metropolitan Museum of Art in New York, organised by Diana Vreeland. Twenty years later, the Fondation Pierre Bergé–Yves Saint Laurent, established in 2002, safeguards 5,000 haute couture and 1,000 SAINT LAURENT *rive gauche* garments, 15,000 accessories and 35,000 drawings that bear witness to Yves Saint Laurent's creativity.

In Marrakech, in the central hall and heart of the Yves Saint Laurent museum, the couturier invites us to undertake another journey, an imaginary one through a lavish universe revealing the underlying influences on his creative vision and the essential emotion and passion communicated through his dresses: from the sands of the Sahara to the imperial court of Russia, from the screen icons of Hollywood to the Impressionist gardens of Proust. This voyage, a dazzling marriage of the intimate and the exceptional, takes place in a setting showcasing the timeless allure of Yves Saint Laurent.

In a scenography that focuses on thematic and emotional impulses, rather than on dates and a chronological presentation, an artist's vision is magnified. This vision is illuminated and rises suddenly to the surface amid a glossary of sensations, distilled in quickly drawn dresses; all are talismans reunited here for the first time, as if in a curiosity cabinet. In this interior Eden, emotional arabesques surge from the artist's gestures; black as well as a universe of colours are employed. Colours that Yves Saint Laurent discovered in Morocco, beginning in 1966, and from which he created an emotional palette and a language dedicated to beauty. **L.B.**

The Yves Saint Laurent
Hall at the musée
YVES SAINT LAURENT
marrakech

*From left to right:*
"Yves Saint Laurent and
Art", "An Invitation to the
Ball", "The Extraordinary
Gardens"

Background audiovisual
projections show details
of the garments.

Scenography:
Christophe Martin
Architects

*"Fashions fade, style is eternal.*
*I dream of offering women the basics*
*of a classic wardrobe that, avoiding*
*the fashion of the moment, will give*
*them more self-confidence.*
*My hope is to make them happier."*

**YVES SAINT LAURENT**

The Yves Saint Laurent Hall

Evening dress.
Haute Couture Collection,
Fall-Winter 1970.
2017 reproduction of the
original wool crepe dress
with back of Chantilly lace

Sailing ensemble.
Haute Couture Collection,
Spring-Summer 1962.
2017 reproduction of
the original wool pea coat.
Shantung blouse and
trousers

In the background,
a portrait of Yves Saint
Laurent by Jeanloup Sieff,
1971

Yves Saint Laurent,
photograph by
Maurice Hogenboom,
1964

# YVES SAINT LAURENT:
# AN ARTISTIC LIFE

Yves Saint Laurent was born in 1936 in Oran, Algeria. He and Pierre Bergé opened the Yves Saint Laurent couture house in Paris in December 1961. No longer welcome at the House of Dior, he not only transformed his name into a brand, he made the brand the symbol of an allure —as expressed in his *rive gauche* style, launched in 1966, and his perfume in 1968— that was distinct and absolute. In his preparatory sketches, Yves Saint Laurent shows faces as well as dresses, revealing the essence of a gesture and the personality of women ready to assert their strength without abandoning emotion; proclaiming their aspirations in the discovery and conquest of a new personal and social power, while never renouncing their power to seduce, and instead totally affirming it.

Alongside Yves Saint Laurent, these women warriors glorify a unique force: each is able to conquer the world by her charm, by her sense of fantasy which reveals itself in a thousand and one ways, exalted by a wardrobe, perfumes, and a line of cosmetics launched in 1978. A citizen of the world, inspired by North Africa as well as by the rest of the continent and Asia, Yves Saint Laurent conveyed fundamental universal values as personified in all his muses: from Zizi Jeanmarie to Catherine Deneuve, from Loulou de la Falaise to Betty Catroux. The 1970s were filled with voyages, while the '80s and '90s revealed his passion for art.

Yves Saint Laurent changed the way women lived, simplifying their lifestyle by designing clothes that borrowed from a masculine wardrobe: the pea coat, the trench coat, the safari jacket, the tuxedo-inspired "smoking", and trousers that were already seen at the unveiling of his first haute couture collection in January 1962. He magnified women's individuality and identity with colours and accessories that adorned garments of an extreme purity, as exemplified in his quickly drawn sketches of draped figures. Long-lasting imprints of black, gold, pink and red are scattered across the couturier's universe, filled with timeless and absolute silhouettes captured by the greatest photographers of his age —Jeanloup Sieff, Helmut Newton, Guy Bourdin. He was a visionary, smashing the stereotypes of vanity. Yves Saint Laurent lived his life in pursuit of beauty, drawing on a cinematic, literary and operatic past, as well as on the colours and sounds of everyday street life, the expressions of passersby, the zeitgeist and all it revealed. He was, as Jean Cocteau defined a poet in his *Secrets de beauté*, "the guardian of an anarchist tradition." **L.B.**

Inaugural collection
at the Yves Saint Laurent
couture house,
Spring-Summer 1962.
This is the first time
we see the "heart" pendant
by Roger Scemama;
it would become
the couturier's talisman.

—

Cover of the French
edition of *Vogue*
(Photograph: Michael
Roberts, 1988)

*"I am not a couturier,*
*only an artisan,*
*a craftsman of joy."*

**YVES SAINT LAURENT**

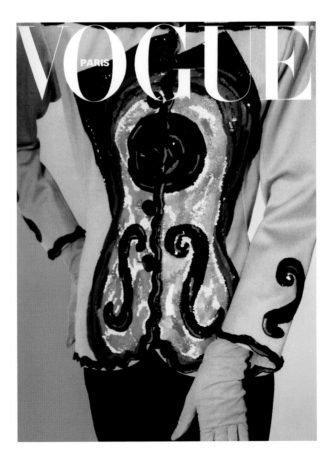

Short version of
"le smoking", modelled
by Danielle Luquet
de Saint Germain.
Haute Couture Collection,
Spring-Summer 1968

—

The "Opéra–Ballets Russes"
Haute Couture Collection,
Spring-Summer 1976
(Photograph:
Patrick Bertrand, 1976)

*"My mother gave me a book on Mondrian
for my birthday. While leafing through its pages,
I imagined that those black lines
could move and follow the contours
of a woman's body without in any way losing
the purity found in Mondrian's paintings.
It was the beginning for me of a long,
creative journey that would find its way to Pop Art,
Warhol, Lichtenstein, Wesselmann…"*

YVES SAINT LAURENT

# MONDRIAN

Yves Saint Laurent declared that "Mondrian is purity, one cannot go any further in painting. The masterpiece of the 20th century is a Mondrian." In July 1965, the Fall-Winter Haute Couture Collection, known as the "Homage to Mondrian" collection, included ten Racine jersey dresses directly inspired by the Dutch artist's 1935 painting *Composition C (Nº III)*. The "Mondrian dresses" that graced the cover of the September 1965 cover of *Elle*, as well as the covers of *Harper's Bazaar* and the French edition of *Vogue*, signalled a graphic and formalistic revolution in the fashion world, and remain, to this day, among the most-copied dresses in history. In the same way that mobiles redefined sculpture, Yves Saint Laurent's "Mondrian dresses" marked a new feminine allure in keeping with the revolutionary spirit of the time. In 1978, Pierre Bergé and Yves Saint Laurent acquired Mondrian's 1922 painting *Composition in Blue, Red, Yellow and Black*. **L.B.**

Worksheet ("bible")
for the dress "Homage
to Piet Mondrian".
Haute Couture Collection,
Fall-Winter 1965

—

Mondrian dress.
Assembled jersey
wool yokes.
Haute Couture Collection,
Fall-Winter 1965

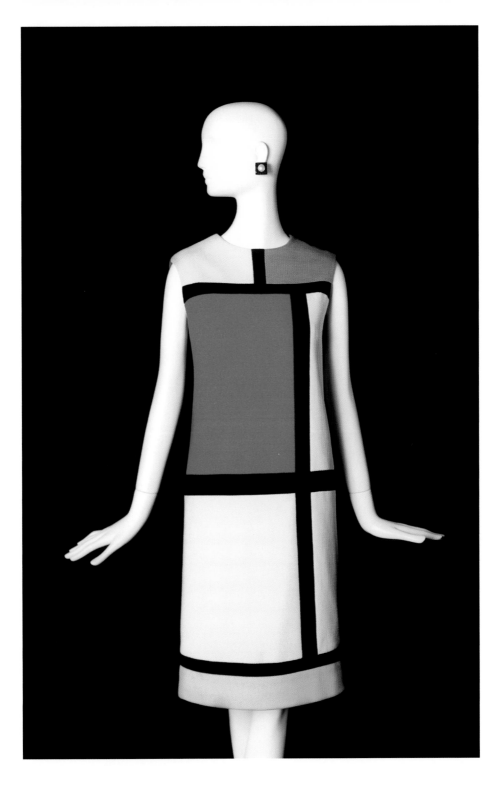

# MASCULINE-FEMININE

Yves Saint Laurent redefined femininity, one freed from all taboos and parodies: "I am searching, for women, the equivalent of a man's business suit." From his first pea coat (1962) to his jumpsuit (1969); from his "smoking" (1966) to his safari jacket (1967), Yves Saint Laurent was inspired by a utilitarian wardrobe, often military in origin, in order to appropriate elements, bend them, and reinvent a vocabulary of style. When his "Il" style was seen in *Elle* magazine, it was clear he had imposed new codes on the fashion world that were timeless, beyond fashion's seasons and trends. **L.B.**

*"When it's pants, it's Yves."*

**LAUREN BACALL**

*"Le smoking" is an essential garment
as it is one of style and not of fashion.
Fashions fade, style is eternal."*

**YVES SAINT LAURENT**

Jumpsuit—"smoking" of grain de poudre wool and silk sateen. SAINT LAURENT *rive gauche*, Spring-Summer 1975

Trench coat of synthetic silk rep. Jacket, vest and tuxedo trousers of grain de poudre wool. SAINT LAURENT *rive gauche*, Spring-Summer 2000

Jacket and trousers of pinstriped wool. Striped silk crepe blouse. SAINT LAURENT *rive gauche*, Spring-Summer 1998

Jacket and Bermuda shorts of grain de poudre wool and silk sateen (Dormeuil fabric). Cigaline and silk sateen blouse (Bucol and Dormeuil fabrics). Haute Couture Collection, Spring-Summer 1986

Worksheet ("bible")
for a "smoking".
Haute Couture Collection,
Spring-Summer 2000

—

"Smoking." Jacket of grain
de poudre wool (Gandini
fabric) with lining of silk
sateen (Helsa fabric).
Trousers of grain de poudre
wool (Gandini fabric)
and silk sateen (Dormeuil
fabric). White cotton
blouse (Stotz fabric).
Haute Couture Collection,
Spring-Summer 2000

Gold-lamé dress with scale
motif (Abraham fabric)
and silk velvet (Hurel fabric).
Brown fox stole.
Haute Couture Collection,
Fall-Winter 1980

Silk velvet floor length
gown (Hurel fabric) with frill
of "cils-dorés" changeant
(shot) silk taffeta against a
gold-lamé background.
(Bucol fabric).
Haute Couture Collection,
Fall-Winter 1978

Goffered gold-lamé
brocade cape (Abraham
fabric). Silk crepe dress
(Taroni fabric).
Haute Couture Collection,
Fall-Winter 1988

*"Gold: because it's the purity
of a flowing spring moulding
the body until
it becomes a single line."*

YVES SAINT LAURENT

*"Black: I love it because it affirms.
It designs, it creates a style:
a woman in a black dress is like
the stroke of a pencil.
But let's be clear: not the 'little black dress'
worn with pearls and a mink stole.
Modern black."*

YVES SAINT LAURENT

# BLACK

This ceremonial colour, one used by the bourgeoisie to codify special occasions, was employed by Yves Saint Laurent as a signature, gesture and seal. As seen in his "smoking" —of grain de poudre wool or draped muslin as if emerging from a quickly-drawn sketch— black is above all an invitation to a sensual realm. It is the imprint of desire, the promise of a multitude of apparitions, expressed by the most opaque to the most transparent of fabrics. For Yves Saint Laurent, black is a single pencil stroke on a white page. A signature gesture. A spirit presenting —exactly and austerely— silhouettes in space, in a calligraphic manner.

In the footsteps of the great stars of Hollywood, Yves Saint Laurent's blacks and whites define an allure; scripted dream-like images emerge from a cinematheque where immaculate minks and gowns press against flesh, providing a masterful lesson of shadow and light.

Black and gold form, in the hands of Yves Saint Laurent —like invitations to roam the vast steppes, crossing "rivers of honey" on horseback alongside fairytale boyars—, otherworldly dreams where odalisques and gypsies travel on uncharted trails, recalling the bronze shield of Genghis Kahn, in a "whirlwind of festivities." **L.B.**

*"My woman is a real woman;*
*she's neither an amazon warrior nor a Barberella;*
*she's not a cosmonaut; she's a woman*
*who is dressed often in black, since I love black*
*and black is my favourite colour; I think a blank sheet*
*of white paper is very boring, and that without black*
*there are no pencil strokes, no lines,*
*and that's why my women are often dressed in black;*
*and I love that they resemble drawings*
*and work sketches."*

YVES SAINT LAURENT

Worksheet ("bible")
for a long evening dress.
Haute Couture Collection,
Spring-Summer 1983

—

Silk velvet dress
(Moreau fabric), draped
belt of leather silk sateen
(Taroni fabric).
Haute Couture Collection,
Fall-Winter 1984

Grain de poudre wool
jacket and trousers
(Laurent Garigue fabric).
Silk sateen blouse
and belt (Taroni fabric).
Haute Couture Collection,
Spring-Summer 1984

# A VISION OF AFRICA

Dreams of capes worn with long dresses; dreams that brave the strongest desert winds; of mirages bathed in browns, and of wild beasts; colours of an Africa rippling with endless dunes. "The sun is never so beautiful as the day one takes to the road…" wrote Jean Giono. The call of the desert, as felt by Yves Saint Laurent, was open to all transformations, to the voluptuousness of space and silence; to raw forms, ebony cuffs, gilded metal collars that invest these nomadic women, draped in silk and cashmere, with an aristocratic presence. **L.B.**

### "BOUGAINVILLEA" CAPE

The violet bougainvillea bursts against the red, cracked wall, a chromatic harmony dear to the couturier, evoking a supernatural nature where expression is magnified rather than imitated, a realm where colours abandon themselves to a dizzying sensation. **L.B.**

Worksheet ("bible")
for the "Bougainvillea" cape.
Haute Couture Collection,
Spring-Summer 1989

M.

71   4405 X

Catherine / Amalia.

Cape de faille rouge
Taroni 1319 Col 911

fleurs de soie de
Mr Lemaire (-violet/rouge)
doublé gazar canard
Abraham 8003/968

4405 bis - robe Catherine
de mousseline -
haut brique
Bianchini 23184/213
ceinture vermillon
Sari's Lajaunian Col 58
jupe vert emeraude
Bianchini 23184/162
fond turquoise
Sari's Lajaunian /80.
B.O. BASCHET (CC 11/B) losange rouge foncé
+ pierres + boules vert jade

escarpins
satin orange

2FM  5/11/87

*"At every street corner in Marrakech,
one stumbles upon striking groups of men
and women, appearing as if in relief:
pink, blue, green and violet caftans blending
with one another. One is surprised that
these groups, which seem drawn or painted and
evoke sketches by Delacroix, are in fact
spontaneous arrangements of everyday life."*

**YVES SAINT LAURENT**

Silk faille cape,
embroidered with silk
organza bougainvillea
flowers and stone beads
(by Lemarié).
Haute Couture Collection,
Spring-Summer 1989
Chiffon dress and belt.
2017 reproduction
of the original

*"Fashion is the reflection of an epoch.*
*This safari jacket was conceived*
*in the same spirit that*
*animated the student uprising*
*of May '68 and the women's liberation*
*movement. It was the age*
*of The Beatles and The Rolling Stones,*
*of an explosive younger generation.*
*It was exhilarating. At the same time,*
*the safari jacket is a classic,*
*a word that doesn't suggest 'boring' to me,*
*but rather something eternal."*

**YVES SAINT LAURENT**

# THE SAFARI JACKET

The linen or cotton safari jacket, with its four military regulation pockets, was worn by the British army in India or members of the Afrika korps. Once reimagined by Yves Saint Laurent, it became a legitimate urban garment, the emblem of the "jungle look" featured by *Vogue* in 1968 through the lens of Franco Rubartelli. His iconic photograph of the model Veruschka wearing an Yves Saint Laurent safari jacket would herald more than a style: it glorified an attitude. The first version, worn by the model Danielle Luquet de Saint Germain, was unveiled in January 1968. Ready-to-wear safari jackets would follow, as well as a pant suit version that sealed forever the couturier's imprint on this classic garment. **L.B.**

Veruschka in a lace-up
safari jacket.
Spring-Summer 1968
Collection.
From the French edition
of *Vogue*, photograph
by Franco Rubartelli

Cotton gabardine safari
jacket and Bermuda shorts.
Haute Couture Collection,
Spring-Summer 1968
(2017 reproduction)

—

Worksheet ("bible")
for the safari jacket.
Haute Couture Collection,
Spring-Summer 1968

*"I imagine lands
that I've never visited, and that's
where I undertake
my most beautiful journeys."*

**YVES SAINT LAURENT**

*"From the terraces and pagodas
of the red pavilion,
I watch my dreams dance on the silvery
water of a river called Love."*

**YVES SAINT LAURENT**

# THE IMAGINARY
# VOYAGES

Travelling became, for Yves Saint Laurent, an invitation to go anywhere, a beautiful escape to the far reaches of dreams, a reality enhanced by expressions and memories. From Morocco to India, from the Spain of Goya to the China of Genghis Khan, Yves Saint Laurent's universe was one of a painter obsessed with the living moment, ready to exalt in his collections the very soul of everything he had loved, seen and felt. Without being an ethnographic excerpt or copy, his style was nourished by all the colours of the world, in an endless creative movement, cosmopolitan and inspired. **L.B.**

Collection board for the
"Opéra – Ballets Russes"
Haute Couture Collection,
Fall- Winter 1976 (detail)

*"Traditional, folkloric costumes*
*have always interested me.*
*First of all because their forms*
*are detached from the world*
*of fashion. And because they are*
*worn by young and older women alike.*
*It's one of the foundations*
*and precepts of my work:*
*that the same article of clothing*
*can be worn by women of any age.*
*And that they all appear young.*
*It's a youthfulness conveyed by the*
*simple manner in which these*
*traditional, rural garments are cut."*

**YVES SAINT LAURENT**

Dress of printed silk
crepe with woven pattern.
Trousers of silk sateen
with woven "rice grain"
pattern. Damask silk belt
(Abraham fabric)

Printed silk sateen tunic
with woven pattern
(Abraham fabric) and silk
cord lining (Trégal fabric).
Sateen trousers
with woven "rice grain"
pattern (Abraham fabric)

Printed silk crepe dress
with woven pattern
and matching silk muslin
veil (Abraham fabric)

Silk velvet vest (Léonard fabric) with Brandenbourg passementerie frog closure (by Denez). Blouse of laméd and printed chiffon (Abraham fabric). Silk faille skirt (Taroni fabric) with silk velvet panel (Léonard fabric)

Silk velvet vest (Gandini fabric) with sable trim (by Garande). Laméd chiffon blouse with Kashmiri motifs (Bianchini fabric) and passementerie rope belt (by Leroux). Silk faille dress (Abraham fabric) and silk velvet ribbon (Rodolphe Simon fabric)

Haute Couture Collection, Fall-Winter 1976, known as the "Opéra–Ballets Russes" collection

—

Rounded jacket of laméd silk sateen (Abraham fabric) with passementerie Brandenbourg frog closure. Silk velvet sheath dress (Moreau fabric)

Rounded jacket of quilted silk (Abraham fabric) with passementerie Brandenbourg frog closure (by Leroux) and silk velvet bow (by Moreau). Silk velvet dress (Moreau fabric)

Haute Couture Collection, Fall-Winter 1994

# THE EXTRAORDINARY GARDENS

From Proust's Balbec to the Orientalist gardens of Tangier, Yves Saint Laurent was inspired by nature, by its thousand and one colours, by its flowers that became the fabric of an embroidered fairytale. It was in Marrakech, according to Yves Saint Laurent, that he first understood the power of colour. Indeed, colour would become an integral element of his work and become one with the evocative bewitchment felt in certain artists' landscapes. At the fleeting boundaries reached by the eternal, Yves Saint Laurent captured the magic of Van Gogh's Irises and Bonnard's bougainvilleas, while carefully reproducing in the movement of adorned bodies the absolute sensation of a dream. **L.B.**

Silk organza dress
with rose print
(Abraham fabric).
Haute Couture Collection,
Fall-Winter 1988.

Worksheet ("bible")
for a long evening dress
and bolero jacket,
Haute Couture Collection,
Fall-Winter 1988

—

Long evening ensembles
with bolero jackets of silk
sateen (Abraham fabric)
and silk velvet (Moreau
fabric), embroidered
with sequins, silk sateen
appliqués and tubular
pearl and stone beads
(by Lesage).
Pasadena wool crepe
dress (Gandini fabric).

Haute Couture Collection,
Spring-Summer 1988

*"I love parties.*
*They are happy occasions:*
*shining, sparkling,*
*effervescent. Champagne flutes,*
*gold candelabras,*
*gilt panelling, gold decorations."*

**YVES SAINT LAURENT**

# AN INVITATION
# TO THE BALL

Proust was his favourite author, Visconti among his most adored film directors. It is no wonder Yves Saint Laurent imbued his dresses with the emotion felt at an evening ball. By making every dress a heroine —from Anna Karenina to Oriane de Guermantes— the couturier magnified a presence inspired by literature, cinema, theatre, and of course, opera. Whether at the Bal de Têtes given by the Baron de Redé, for which he designed many of the head-dresses, to the Bal Proust given by Marie-Hélène de Rothschild, Yves Saint Laurent was fascinated in resurrecting times gone by, where passionately induced, magical creatures and spells —time-less and infinitely present— would find themselves invited to the *hôtel particulier* of an artist of emotions. **L.B.**

Watered silk taffeta dress
(Abraham fabric).
Haute Couture Collection,
Fall-Winter 1990

**63**

Worksheet ("bible") for a ball gown. Domino robe of changeant (shot) silk faille (Bucol fabric) and silk velvet (Hurel fabric). Dress of changeant (shot) silk taffeta (Bucol fabric)

Haute Couture Collection, Fall-Winter 2000

—

Dress of satin-silk leather (Abraham fabric) embroidered with lace, sequins and stone bead fringe (by Lesage)

Top of satin-leather silk (Abraham fabric) embroidered with stone bead fringe (by Cécile Henry). Skirt of "flame leather" silk sateen (Taroni fabric).
Haute Couture Collection, Fall-Winter 1991

*"As if it were a river, my imagination
has, over time, swept up music,
painting, sculpture and literature,
even what Nietzsche called
the aesthetic phenomenon without which
life would be unbearable; they are phantoms
which protect my existence
and are manifested in my collections."*

**YVES SAINT LAURENT**

# YVES SAINT LAURENT
# AND ART

In 1956, Georges Braque said "…I saw large birds fly overhead, which led me to imagine aerial forms." Three decades later, Yves Saint Laurent paid homage to him by designing capes embroidered with Cubist doves, as if he were inviting them to take flight over women's bodies draped with muslin or crepe, generating a remarkable conversation between art, fashion and life. **L.B.**

Collection board
for the "Braque"
Haute Couture Collection,
Fall-Winter 1989 (detail)

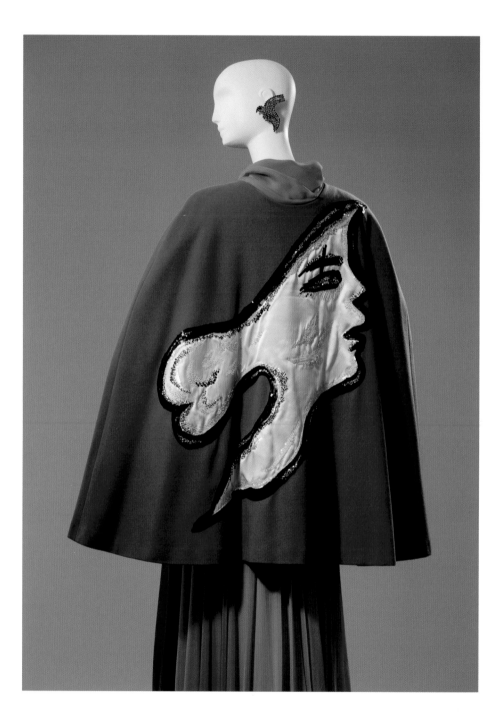

Woolen cloth cape (Garigue
fabric) embroidered
with a Cubist-inspired silk
sateen appliqué,
sequins and tubular pearls
(by Lesage). Laparisian silk
muslin dress (Saris fabric).
Haute Couture Collection,
Spring-Summer 1988

—

The Cubist Cape.
Worksheet ("bible") for
a long evening ensemble
–"Homage to Georges
Braque". Haute Couture
Collection, Spring-
Summer 1988

"The Irises" evening jacket
–"Homage to Vincent van
Gogh"– embroidered
with sequins, tubular and
stone beads and silk organza
ribbons (by Lesage).
Haute Couture Collection,
Spring- Summer 1988

Worksheet ("bible")
for a long evening dress
–"Homage to Georges
Braque". Haute Couture
Collection, Spring-
Summer 1988

The "Heart", 1962.
Three-piece heart-shaped
pendant, covered with
several hundred smoky
grey rhinestones, red
crystal cabochons and
white pearls from
which hangs a drop made
of red glass paste.

# THE CURIOSITY CABINET

Flamboyant, provocative, magical, as if suddenly appearing from a souk or a palace. Or from a fairytale or a jewel-filled chest. A talisman made of wheat or rock crystal. Dreamlike slippers. Barbarian sleeves. Rigid necklaces of hammered metal. Coral cabochons. Exotic wood, lacquered *Opium* inro worn as pendants. Mirrors reflecting passion. Seductive promises.

Accessories, in the hands of Yves Saint Laurent, become charms, fetishistic objects to be worn a thousand different ways, during the day or in the evening, to accentuate a gesture or silhouette. To bewitch everyday life, to change bearing as would a chameleon, with as many materials as there are emotions or royal brooches from a resurrected Golconda. The absolute monarch of this imaginary realm is Yves Saint Laurent's heart talisman, covered with costume diamonds and rubies, pinned every season on his favourite as a sign of love. Sparks given off by life itself —, in all its brilliance and force— the accessories are emblems of Yves Saint Laurent's women who radiate from his spirit, one of fire and ice. One after the other: blond, brunette, red-headed, with diaphanous or ebony skin, on which every ring, every necklace, every pair of earrings becomes adornment. The overpowering presence of fashion trophies, good luck charms, barbarian amulets or neoclassical pearls borrowed from a painter's favourite model illuminate life with a thousand Yves Saint Laurent suns.

In order to glow, to resonate, to affirm one's character; to add to a sweater or "smoking", as simply as with a pencil stroke, an eloquent gesture and the sonorous poetry of movement; to play with every one of life's moments, whether in jeans or an evening dress. Yves Saint Laurent drew upon Moroccan traditions to find his talismans: fez, gandouras, corded belts, sarouel trousers, and hammered metal Berber jewellery. As if there and everywhere they appear, his accessories —from the most Baroque to the most sleekly refined— adhere to the same objective: be above all the bearers of light. **L.B.**

"Bambara" dress of silk
organza embroidered
with rhodoïd, wooden
and stone beads
(Lanel by Lesage).
Haute Couture Collection,
Spring-Summer 1967

Long evening dress
Haute Couture Collection,
Fall-Winter 1969.
Blue crepe voile with
galvanised copper chest
sculpture by Claude Lalanne

Long evening dress
Haute Couture Collection,
Fall-Winter 1969.
Black crepe voile with
black organza lining and
galvanised copper waist
sculpture by Claude Lalanne

*"It pleases me to think that in Marrakech,
in a Moroccan oasis and a stone's throw
from the Jardin Majorelle,
a cultural centre named after Yves Saint Laurent
exists, housing a museum, auditorium,
and library, and which,
while remaining true to its ancestral roots,
looks proudly towards the future."*

PIERRE BERGÉ

# MUSEUM ARCHITECTURE

Every project tells a story; one written with architecture. Every story has its setting, protagonists and authors. Yves Saint Laurent is this story's leading character, along with Pierre Bergé, who dreamed of a building worthy of the couturier's iconic work; in his own words, "a structure both contemporary and profoundly Moroccan." The setting was obvious: Marrakech, the Moroccan city where the fashion designer would often stay to reflect, gather his creative strength, and find inspiration.

Located a short distance down the Rue Yves Saint Laurent from the legendary Jardin Majorelle, the building distinguishes itself by volumes and material that simultaneously express a modern spirit and strong attachment to Morocco. Its exterior architecture is opaque, abstract and mysterious. One is reminded of the fragile nature of the collections it houses, highly sensitive to light, but also of the traditional, windowless houses of the medina of Marrakech.

Contrasting volumes are assembled to compose an architecture where one deduces the different activities of the museum. The building seems to rise from the earth, as if draped; its base is surfaced with a granito made from shards of Moroccan marble and stone. While the granito used for the base is rugged and coarse, one's hand discovers the smoothness of the walls. Terra cotta bricks animate the higher portions of the walls, forming a lacework of different motifs; one notes the refined brick-laying employed. The generous Moroccan sun creates shadows that extend and shift throughout the day, forming ever-changing patterns. The colour so particular to Marrakech dominates the overall building, allowing it to blend harmoniously with the palette of the Red City.

musée
YVES SAINT LAURENT
marrakech : southern
facade of the building

Guests enter the museum by a circular courtyard, open to the sky, where they can pause and clear their minds —as if in a decompression chamber— before entering the exhibition halls. Its convex walls are punctuated by stained-glass windows echoing the work of Matisse and that of the couturier; they act as fissures, diffusing soft, coloured rays of light throughout the interior. Adjoining the courtyard is a square-shaped patio; its bluish-green hue, restrained yet luminous at the same time, is achieved by hundreds of enamelled bricks. It provides plentiful light to the Grand Hall. It's from there, the heart of the building, that visitors discover the exhibition halls, the boutique and café, as well as the auditorium and library.

Basic round and square forms perfectly express the contrasts articulated in the museum: a constant dialogue between straight and curved lines, open and closed spaces, light and darkness, rough and smooth surfaces. Working together, they effortlessly awaken a self-evident elegance that permeates the building.

**KARL FOURNIER ET OLIVIER MARTY,**
STUDIO KO

musée
YVES SAINT LAURENT
marrakech :
the circular patio at night

—

musée
YVES SAINT LAURENT
marrakech :
the square interior patio,
fountain with sidewalls
covered with green *zelliges*

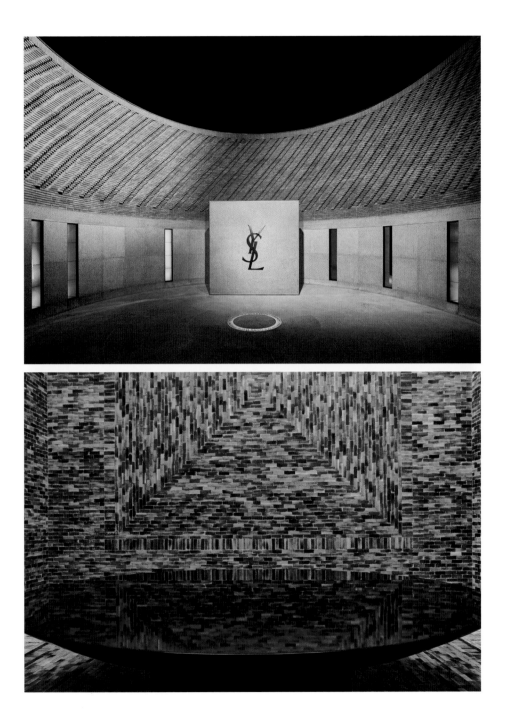

musée YVES SAINT LAURENT
marrakech : east facade
and main entrance
on the Rue Yves Saint Laurent

Mon truc en
palmes

# CULTURAL PROGRAMMING

More than just a museum, the musée YVES SAINT LAURENT marrakech is a cultural centre accessible to a broad public: of course to tourists visiting the Jardin Majorelle, but also to residents of Marrakech and citizens of Morocco. A dynamic cultural programming takes advantage of various museum venues: the hall for temporary exhibitions, the gallery and theatre lobby, the Pierre Bergé Auditorium and the museum's research library.

### TEMPORARY EXHIBITION HALL

Conceived as a dynamic cultural aperture, this space is the setting for diverse exhibitions —two or three per year— related to art, contemporary art and design, fashion, anthropology and botany.

### THE GALLERY

Every year, the museum's gallery will highlight work by a photographer who worked with Yves Saint Laurent. Many renowned photographers of the second half of the 20th century —including Pierre Boulat, Helmut Newton, André Rau and Jeanloup Sieff— contributed to the fame and prestige of the couture house; the gallery bears witness to their precious collaboration with the couturier.

### THE THEATRE LOBBY

Here one sees the important work done by Yves Saint Laurent for the theatre, ballet, cabaret and cinema. From the beginning of the 1950s until the end of his career, the couturier was greatly influenced by the stage and screen, as seen by a selection of sketches, drawings and photographs of costumes he designed.

Catherine Deneuve
in the medina of Marrakech,
photographed in 1992
by André Rau for the French
edition of *Elle*. The dove
motif on the embroidered
cape she is wearing was
inspired by Braque.
Haute Couture Collection,
Spring-Summer 1988

The Pierre Bergé
Auditorium, musée
YVES SAINT LAURENT
marrakech

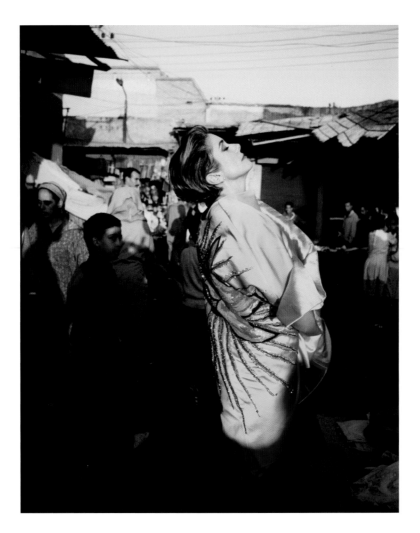

### THE PIERRE BERGÉ AUDITORIUM

This 150-seat auditorium adapts itself to the diverse needs of the museum. A state-of-the-art, modular acoustics system is employed for the projection of films and documentaries on Yves Saint Laurent as well as a broader film programming, live concerts, live broadcasts of operas and theatre from around the world, conferences and colloquiums.

## THE LIBRARY

The library's collection, including over 5,000 volumes related to Arabo-Andalusian and Berber culture, botany, costume history and fashion can be consulted by researchers and the general public by appointment.

## THE BOOKSHOP

The museum's bookshop was inspired by the first ready-to-wear boutique, SAINT LAURENT *rive gauche*, which opened in Paris in 1966. Here one finds volumes related to Yves Saint Laurent, fashion and Morocco, or work shown in the temporary exhibition hall. The couturier's presence is felt in the posters and his iconic LOVE postcards.

## LE STUDIO CAFÉ

The museum's café, Le Studio, takes its name from Yves Saint Laurent's workspace at the couture house on Avenue Marceau in Paris and evokes the calm and intimate environment where the couturier would retreat and work. The menu offers traditional Moroccan and inventive French dishes that take advantage of the best quality local ingredients and produce.

Research Library, musée
YVES SAINT LAURENT
marrakech.

From 1976 to 2002,
the Yves Saint Laurent
couture house was located
at 5 Avenue Marceau
in Paris. The building
today houses the Musée
Yves Saint Laurent Paris.

# MUSÉE YVES SAINT LAURENT PARIS

Yves Saint Laurent (1936-2008) and Pierre Bergé (1930-2017) met in 1958. In 1961, they decided to establish their own couture house; the first collection was presented on 29 January 1962 at 30 bis Rue Spontini in Paris. In 1974, the couture house moved to new quarters: a Napoleon III-style *hôtel particulier* at 5 Avenue Marceau in Paris. It is here that the Musée Yves Saint Laurent opens its doors to the public, showcasing the couturier's work in a historic building that was the centre of the Yves Saint Laurent universe. A permanent, theme-based collection and temporary exhibitions allow visitors the opportunity to understand the overall work of the renowned fashion designer. The goal of the museum's programming is to ensure a cohesive dialogue between the different areas of museum while highlighting prototype couture garments prepared for the runway shows. These unique pieces, created under the supervision of Yves Saint Laurent, are in an exemplary state of conservation.

The opening of the Musée Yves Saint Laurent Paris is in line with a worldwide trend by fashion houses to conserve and restore their archives. Its collection nevertheless stands out, as Yves Saint Laurent was the first living fashion designer to keep his prototypes for safekeeping. The idea of conserving his work came to the couturier in 1964, the day following the runway shows, when he chose which prototypes should be set aside and kept for posterity. In 1982, he began writing "museum" on certain worksheets used by his team, indicating pieces that should be conserved and eventually moved to the couture house's archives, which were established in 1997.

To understand the birth of a collection, one should study its history and the creative process behind the prototypes it houses. The couturier's sketch is the starting point for all that follows. Beginning in 1966, Yves Saint Laurent began drawing his collections in Marrakech, Morocco; his discovery of the country and its gardens was an absolute revelation for the couturier, particularly in the range of colours he would employ. His work shown at the musée YVES SAINT LAURENT marrakech is thus seen in a special setting and context: in the country that enchanted him, and a stone's throw from the garden from which he drew such inspiration. It is definitely here, in Marrakech, that he undertook one of his rare "non-imaginary" voyages, and it is here, in contact with one of his greatest and most direct sources of inspiration, that we should begin approaching the work of this artist.

**AURÉLIE SAMUEL,**
DIRECTOR AND CURATOR OF THE COLLECTIONS
AT THE MUSÉE YVES SAINT LAURENT, PARIS

"LOVE" greeting card, 1986
Designed by
Yves Saint Laurent,
the cards were sent every
year to clients of the
couture house and friends.

## MUSÉE YVES SAINT LAURENT MARRAKECH
## FONDATION JARDIN MAJORELLE

## ADVISORY BOARD OF THE YSL MUSEUMS IN PARIS AND MARRAKECH

**LAURENCE BENAÏM**
Journalist and author
of several books on
Yves Saint Laurent including
his biography (Grasset,
1993), *Yves Saint Laurent,
Début*, with photographs by
Pierre Boulat (La Martinière,
2002) and *Dior / Yves Saint
Laurent* (Assouline, 2017),
Laurence Benaïm worked
alongside Dominique
Deroche and the museum's
Advisory Board in choosing
the dresses exhibited
at the musée YVES SAINT
LAURENT marrakech.

**FATIMA ZAHRA MOKHTARI**
Editorial Manager
The Fondation
Jardin Majorelle

—

Graphic Design
Philippe Apeloig
assisted by Yannick James

Translation
José Abete

Printer
Direct Print, Casablanca

Typography
Effra, Renard

Photoengraving
Les Artisans du Regard,
Paris

Legal Deposit
2017MO3836

ISBN
978-9954-9179-5-4

Cover:
Yves Saint Laurent at
work, Villa Dar Es Saada,
Marrakech
(Photograph: Pierre
Boulat)

**musée**
# YVES SAINT LAURENT
**marrakech**

Rue Yves Saint Laurent
Marrakech, Morocco
+ 212 (0)5242-98686
www.museeyslmarrakech.com

Open every day from 10am to 6pm
exept Wednesdays